The Road to Seneca Falls

The Road to Seneca Falls

A Story about Elizabeth Cady Stanton

by Gwenyth Swain

illustrations by Mary O'Keefe Young

A Carolrhoda Creative Minds Book

Carolrhoda Books, Inc./Minneapolis

To the memory of
Margaret Hutchinson Coman

This book is available in two editions:
Library binding by Carolrhoda Books, Inc.
Soft cover by First Avenue Editions
c/o The Lerner Group
241 First Avenue North
Minneapolis, Minnesota 55401

Library of Congress Cataloging-in-Publication Data

Swain, Gwenyth.
    The road to Seneca Falls : a story about Elizabeth Cady Stanton / by
Gwenyth Swain ; illustrations by Mary O'Keefe Young.
        p.   cm. — (A Carolrhoda creative minds book)
    Includes bibliographical references and index.
    Summary: A biography of suffragist Elizabeth Cady Stanton, one of the
organizers of the country's first women's rights convention, which took place
in Seneca Falls, New York, in 1848.
    ISBN 0-87614-947-6 (lib. bdg.)
    ISBN 1-57505-025-0 (pbk.)
    1. Stanton, Elizabeth Cady, 1815–1902—Juvenile literature. 2. Feminists—
United States—Biography—Juvenile literature. 3. Suffragists—United
States—Biography—Juvenile literature. 4. Women's rights—United States—
History—Juvenile literature. 5. Women—Suffrage—United States—
History—Juvenile literature. [1. Stanton, Elizabeth Cady, 1815–1902.
2. Feminists. 3. Women—Biography. 4. Women's rights—History.]
I. Young, Mary O'Keefe, ill. II. Title. III. Series.
HQ1413.S67S93   1996
305.42'092—dc20
[B]   96-7387

Manufactured in the United States of America
1 2 3 4 5 6 – MA – 01 00 99 98 97 96

Table of Contents

(1)

To Be a Boy!

I commenced the struggle of life
under favorable circumstances
on the 12th day of November, 1815.
—Elizabeth Cady Stanton

"I tell you what to do," said Margaret Cady to her older sister Elizabeth. "Hereafter, let us act as we choose, without asking."

At first Elizabeth thought Madge's idea was wonderful, but she soon realized there might be problems. "Then," she told Madge, "we shall be punished."

"Suppose we are," Madge answered. "We shall have had our fun at any rate, and that is better than to mind the everlasting 'no' and not have any fun at all."

Madge had a point, Elizabeth decided. At school the teacher said no whenever Elizabeth recited her lessons out of turn. On Sundays in the cold Presbyterian church on the hill, all the commandments started with "Thou shalt not . . ." And in the Cady's very proper home, an everlasting no seemed to meet Elizabeth at every turn, just when she was beginning to enjoy herself.

Children, Elizabeth had been told many times, were meant to be seen and not heard. And girls were meant to be practically invisible—at least that's how it felt to Elizabeth when she or one of her sisters was sent to Judge Cady's office for quiet time. Or when they weren't allowed to slide down the woodpile in winter. Or when the nursemaid told them not to play blindman's bluff in the cellar.

Perhaps Elizabeth had heard one "no" too many, for she found herself agreeing with her younger sister. Together, eight-year-old Elizabeth and six-year-old Madge began to do what they wanted, even when it meant trouble.

To Elizabeth's delight, there was almost no limit to what she could do, or what trouble she could get into, growing up in Johnstown, New York. In the 1820s, Johnstown was not a very large town nor a very pretty one—Elizabeth thought it was a downright gloomy place on gray winter days. But home was right at the center of things on the town square, and that was an exciting place to be.

The Cady family's white frame house was one of the biggest in Johnstown. It was only just big enough to hold Elizabeth, her parents, and her sisters, Tryphena, Harriet, Margaret (nicknamed Madge), and Catherine, or Cate. Then there was the nurse-maid, a handful of other servants, young law students, and Elizabeth's older brother, Eleazar, who stayed at the house when he wasn't in school. People were always coming and going, since Judge Cady was a practicing lawyer and had an office on the ground floor.

Elizabeth's favorite hideaway was two floors above. From a high, round attic window, she surveyed Johnstown and the hilly countryside of north central New York. In the attic, Elizabeth and her sisters emptied the trunks of old clothes for playing dress up. They snatched bits of maple sugar from the crumbling cakes stored on a shelf. And they whirled the old spinning wheels around until their arms were worn out. None of the Cady children were allowed in the attic, so they went there as often as they could—especially after Elizabeth stopped worrying about older people who said no.

At about the time the two sisters had their talk, Madge joined Elizabeth and Harriet on the daily walk to and from Maria Yost's grammar school. Cate, the baby, was still too young for school, while Tryphena was already graduated. Mrs. Cady outfitted the three girls in red from head to toe, all the way down to bright red, scratchy stockings. Elizabeth was sure they all stuck out like sore thumbs. Still, when she wasn't thinking of ways to persuade her mother to let her wear a dress of a different color, she enjoyed school. Elizabeth and her sisters learned reading, writing, and grammar, and all the other things Miss Yost felt young girls needed to know.

In 1826, when Elizabeth was eleven, her brother Eleazar graduated from Union College in Schenectady, New York. Eleazar was nearly ten years older than Elizabeth. Elizabeth didn't know him well, since he was often away from home. But now that Eleazar was returning, the house was full of anticipation.

The only boy in the family, Eleazar was his parents' favorite child. He would carry on the Cady name. And being the only boy, he alone of the Cady children could have a career. Eleazar planned to study under his father. He was to follow in Judge Cady's footsteps and become a lawyer, perhaps even a judge. But those plans remained only plans. The family had barely welcomed Eleazar home when he became ill and died.

After Eleazar's death, Judge Cady sat wordlessly for hours. Mrs. Cady pulled out the trunks of old baby clothes and thought about having another son. The family had known death before, but they never grew used to it. Besides Eleazar, three other sons had died in childhood, one just months before Elizabeth was born. The Cadys' first child, a daughter, had also died young. Death, especially among young people, was common then, when doctors had few medicines for treating diseases. But being common didn't make death easier to accept.

Servants draped the doorways with black crepe and covered all the mirrors. The five Cady sisters kept their voices down without being told, and they were careful not to bang doors. The older girls made sure baby Cate stayed out of trouble.

On the day before the funeral, Eleazar's body lay in a casket in the darkened parlor. Elizabeth looked in and found her father sitting there, so lost in thought that he didn't see her. When she sat on his knee, he hardly seemed to notice. But then he sighed and said, "Oh, my daughter, I wish you were a boy!"

Elizabeth would gladly have done anything to make her father happy, but being a girl was one thing she couldn't change. She remembered when her sister Cate was born and the neighbors had all said, Oh, what a pity the baby is a girl. Elizabeth had noticed that people in general preferred boys to girls, but she didn't know precisely why. Now she was determined to find out.

That night she considered the question from all sides. What was it that made boys better than girls? she wondered. Mainly, Elizabeth decided, boys knew more than girls and had more spunk, more courage.

The next morning, she awoke with a plan. Before her brother's body was taken to the church for the funeral, Elizabeth walked through the dewy grass to the house next door. The Reverend Simon Hosack, a retired minister, answered Elizabeth's knock. Would he teach her Greek?

Certainly, he replied. They could begin immediately.

But learning Greek was only part of Elizabeth's plan. To make herself more courageous, she put aside her fears and learned to handle a horse. Before long she was driving the family's carriage and riding well enough to jump ditches.

And as soon as she could, Elizabeth asked her parents to let her take classes at Johnstown Academy. (Unlike most high schools in those days, the academy admitted girls as well as boys.) There, Elizabeth

13

could study Latin, Greek, and mathematics with the boys who planned to go to college.

If Elizabeth had needed an example of a woman who was as brave and intelligent as any boy or man, she could have found one in her mother. Just under six feet tall, Margaret Livingston Cady rode horseback often and well. She was independent and brave. In the household, she alone stood up to Judge Cady. Margaret made sure her husband, Daniel, knew her views on everything from where the family should live (in town on the square and not on a farm) to whether they should have rocking chairs on the porch (she approved; he didn't). Mrs. Cady was well educated and encouraged Elizabeth to read. Yet Elizabeth wasn't close to her mother. When she looked for someone she wanted to be like and wanted to please, she looked to her father.

After three years of hard work at the academy, Elizabeth had something she felt sure would impress her father—she had won an important prize for Greek. When she rushed into her father's office, Elizabeth half expected him to say, Well, a girl can be as good as a boy after all! Judge Cady took the prize, a book, in his hands and read the inscription from Elizabeth's teacher. Finally he kissed her on the top of her forehead and said, "Ah, you should have been a boy!"

If Elizabeth hadn't worked so hard to be courageous, she might have been discouraged. But she
dried her tears before dinner. She was braver and
smarter than she had been only a few years before
when her brother died. Though her parents still
grieved for their lost son, Elizabeth and her sisters
were finding new interests and new friends to ease
the pain.

② Looking for Answers

At about the time Eleazar died, two of his former classmates from Union College had come to study law under Judge Cady. Henry Bayard was a practical joker, while his brother Edward was a good listener and a charmer. (Before long Edward married Elizabeth's oldest sister, Tryphena.) Both Bayards spent most of their spare time with the Cady girls.

The first years of Edward and Henry's stay at the Cady house were a blur of horse rides, chess and checkers, picnics . . . and lessons. Because the Bayard brothers were training to be lawyers, they liked to quiz Elizabeth on points of law. Her father was the most famous judge and lawyer in the region, and Elizabeth had often watched him arguing a case in court or giving out legal advice in his office.

At first Elizabeth had only gone to Judge Cady's office when she had to. Whenever she became too much for her mother to handle, she was sent to sit quietly in one of the office chairs. But before long

Elizabeth was coming to the office even when she hadn't done anything wrong.

She loved to listen to her father advising his clients. And she liked to keep the law students from their work with her chatter. She even enjoyed reading her father's tall volumes of the laws of the state of New York.

Elizabeth knew her father was a fine lawyer and an impressive judge. But when Judge Cady looked in his law books, he didn't always have what Elizabeth thought were good enough answers to his clients' questions.

One day when Elizabeth had been sent to the office, Mrs. Flora Campbell arrived in her large hooded coat, a basket over one arm. Flora came almost every week to the Cady house with eggs, maple sugar, a chicken or two, and other goods to sell from her farm just outside Johnstown. Flora had lived on the farm for many years. But now, she told Judge Cady, she hardly felt welcome there at all.

Since Flora's husband had died, her son had become owner of the farm and everything on it. He'd made it clear to Flora that she was there as a guest and should be glad of his kindness. He didn't seem to remember that the farm had been bought with Flora's money and that she had put many years of hard work into making it a success. What should she do? Couldn't Judge Cady help her?

Elizabeth wondered too. Flora was their friend. Surely her father would know what to do. But Judge Cady could only shake his head. The trouble, he explained, was that the law was in the way.

In New York, a married woman couldn't have money or own property of her own. Anything she might have had before her marriage belonged to her husband as soon as she said "I do." When Flora had married, her money had become her husband's money. He had used it to buy the farm and then he had left the farm to their son in his will. According to the law, the farm had never been Flora's farm. Her son could throw her out tomorrow and no one could do a thing about it.

After Flora left, Elizabeth turned to her father. If he couldn't help Flora, wasn't there some way she could?

Judge Cady told his daughter the same thing he would have told one of his students. The laws, he explained, were made at the state legislature in Albany. One had only to go to the legislature as a representative, just as he had done when the people voted for him in 1808. Or a person could go and talk to the representatives and try to persuade them to make the changes that were needed.

That was fine for her father or even for Edward and Henry Bayard, but Elizabeth knew that women couldn't vote, let alone win election to the legislature. And it was not proper, most people said, for a woman to speak in public, particularly in front of a group of men. Good heavens, most restaurants wouldn't even serve a woman eating alone!

Still, Elizabeth meant to find a way to change the laws that were unfair to Flora Campbell. She made sure to ask her father to show her all the laws that made women cry. And she never missed a chance to debate those laws with the students in her father's office. She hoped she might be able to convince one or two of the men to share her views. But mainly her concern for women and for fairness made the law students laugh. Elizabeth was so serious that they found it hard not to make her the butt of their jokes.

One Christmas, Elizabeth was given a beautiful necklace and matching bracelet in glowing red coral. She proudly wore them into the law office the next day, fishing for compliments. Instead, the students teased her mercilessly.

"Now, if in due time you should be my wife," Henry Bayard began, "those ornaments would be mine; I could take them and lock them up, and you could never wear them except with my permission."

Elizabeth tossed her curls and stamped her feet in frustration, but Henry went on. "I could even exchange them for a box of cigars," he said, taking an imaginary puff, "and you could watch them evaporate in smoke."

Henry could be unbearable. But Elizabeth was sad to see him leave in 1829 when he finished his law studies. Edward and Tryphena Bayard stayed on at the Cady home. The couple had no children and spoiled Elizabeth and her younger sisters. Edward was only ten years older than Elizabeth and gradually became a close friend.

When Elizabeth graduated from Johnstown Academy at the age of fifteen, she dreamed of going to Union College, where Edward Bayard and her brother, Eleazar, had studied. But Elizabeth knew it was just a dream. In 1830 no college in the United States admitted women, not Union College, not Yale, not Harvard.

Elizabeth had always been at the top of her class. But she could only wave and say good luck to the boys who boarded the stagecoach for college that fall. Watching her former classmates in their stiff new suits, Elizabeth scuffed her old brown boot on the wooden sidewalk on Main Street.

At Johnstown Academy, she had proven herself the

equal of any boy in Greek, Latin, or math. Yet where would that take her? Judge Cady thought Elizabeth should stay at home and learn to make puddings. Or if she needed some fun, she could go along with him on his rounds as a circuit court judge. There were always dinner parties and balls during the court sessions, and she might meet a nice young man.

Elizabeth tried to do as her father wished, but she wasn't happy. Finally she confided in Edward, and he in turn helped convince the judge that a little more schooling couldn't do Elizabeth any harm.

New Adventures

On January 2, 1831, Elizabeth enrolled as a student at Troy Female Seminary, some forty miles from Johnstown on the Hudson River. The school, started in 1821 by Mrs. Emma Willard, was unusual and quite famous.

Troy Seminary was no finishing school meant to prepare girls for lives as proper ladies and hostesses. Instead, it was nearly a college—or as close to a college as Elizabeth could hope to come. While most finishing schools taught manners and needlework, Troy offered courses in botany, logic, geometry, French, chemistry, piano, and history.

Students were expected to take their schoolwork seriously. The seminary catalog warned that only plain calico and gingham dresses were allowed. Elizabeth was forbidden to pack the lovely coral necklace and bracelet or her fancy lace dress collars. Without these distractions, she and the other girls could concentrate on becoming educated young women.

After years of studying alongside boys, Elizabeth found it hard to adjust to being surrounded by girls. She also missed home cooking. At Troy, dinners were corned beef, liver, or bread pudding followed by corned beef, liver, or bread pudding.

Still, Elizabeth learned a great deal and she grew to admire Emma Willard. In 1819 Mrs. Willard had done what few women dared. She had presented the state legislature in Albany with a plan. Mrs. Willard dreamed of opening a school for girls, and she expected the state's help and money to do it. The lawmakers turned her down, but the town of Troy raised enough money to start the seminary.

By 1833 Elizabeth had learned as much as she could at Emma Willard's school. She returned home to Johnstown no more certain about her future at seventeen than she had been two years before. But before long she had settled down to baking puddings and going to balls and parties—the things a young woman was supposed to do in the 1830s while waiting to meet a young man and marry.

Young men liked Elizabeth Cady, with her dark curls and flashing eyes. She was short—just under five feet tall—and more than a little plump. But what most men remembered about her was her sense of humor. One young man never forgot it.

He bet Elizabeth that she couldn't go for a carriage ride with him and keep quiet. Elizabeth loved to talk (she could hardly stop herself from chattering at times) and she knew it would be hard to hold her tongue. Still, she didn't want to lose a bet.

On the appointed day, the man stepped into the carriage and Elizabeth stayed quiet, unnaturally quiet. After the ride was over, the young man discovered that "Elizabeth" was a dressmaker's dummy wearing a very large hat!

When Elizabeth received her first serious proposal of marriage, it wasn't nearly so much fun. In fact, it stunned her. She had to keep it a secret from everyone because it came from her brother-in-law Edward Bayard. When he confessed his love to her, Elizabeth was more than a little frightened. She knew she loved Edward just as much as he loved her.

Elizabeth may have been tempted to run away with Edward as he urged her to do. But she loved her sister and knew how deeply Tryphena would be hurt.

Once Elizabeth made up her mind to say no to Edward, she set about putting some distance between the two of them. (For his part, Edward Bayard never allowed himself to be alone in a room with Elizabeth Cady for the rest of his life.) Whenever an opportunity arose for Elizabeth to leave Johnstown, she did.

Most often she went to the home of Gerrit Smith, her mother's cousin.

A wealthy man, Smith lived with his family outside Peterboro, New York. His father had founded the village, and Gerrit still owned most of the land for miles around it. But Smith wasn't interested in impressing others with his wealth. He tried to live in such a way that any visitor, no matter how poor, would feel comfortable and welcome in his house.

Some of Gerrit Smith's guests were very poor indeed. They had left their homes and all they knew behind them, hoping to find freedom from slavery. Smith's visitors were escaped southern slaves traveling on the Underground Railroad. This secret network of safe houses stretched from states in the South, where black people could be owned as slaves, to Canada in the North, where slavery was against the law. Gerrit Smith's house was just one "station" on the railroad.

Along with slaves, whose visits were secret, Smith invited other, more public, guests. Peterboro was far from any large town, so Smith brought in his entertainment—a constant stream of reformers, politicians, and preachers. The Smith house was always full of lively debating, something Elizabeth loved. She was also fond of Libby, the Smiths' oldest daughter.

In 1839, when Elizabeth was twenty-three years old, she found another reason to value her visits to Peterboro. That fall, while the leaves turned and the days grew shorter, Elizabeth Cady got to know Henry Brewster Stanton.

Stanton was in the area to lecture on slavery. Like his host Gerrit Smith, Henry Stanton was a firm believer in abolition, or the campaign to end slavery. Since 1835 Stanton had been a member of the Band of Seventy, a handpicked group of the finest and fieriest speakers on abolition. Henry and the other sixty-nine fanned out across the Northeast giving speeches, getting signatures on antislavery petitions, and helping people in small towns set up their own abolitionist groups.

During the fall of 1839, Henry Stanton also managed to fit into his schedule a number of long talks and horseback rides with Elizabeth Cady. When he proposed to her, she didn't believe it at first: she thought Henry was engaged to another guest at the Smith house.

Elizabeth didn't take long to consider and accept Henry's marriage proposal. Ten years older than Elizabeth, Henry Stanton was similar in age and character to Edward Bayard. But Henry's love would not cause others pain.

Marrying Henry would be a daring move for Elizabeth. During her visits to the Smiths, she had been swept off her feet by Henry and by the abolition movement. She knew Judge Cady was opposed to abolition. And she suspected that her father would take a dim view of a man who earned his living lecturing on slavery. She was right.

When Judge Cady heard of Elizabeth's engagement, he insisted that she break it off. For a while she held her ground. But when Edward Bayard joined forces with her father, Elizabeth gave in. In February 1840, she broke her engagement.

Henry Stanton didn't give up. He kept after Elizabeth with the same energy he gave to abolition. For the rest of the winter and on into spring, Henry sent regular letters, posted from different points on his lecture tour.

In one letter, Henry announced that he would be traveling to the World Anti-Slavery Convention in London that June. Leaders of abolition movements in Great Britain, America, and other countries were gathering. Henry would be an official delegate. Elizabeth felt she couldn't bear being separated from Henry for the months of his trip. And she couldn't bear passing up the chance to attend the convention and become part of a great movement.

Elizabeth wrote back insisting that they marry before Henry left for London. Keeping their plans secret, the two met and married in Johnstown on May 1, 1840. Elizabeth meant to be an equal partner with Henry. At their wedding, she made the minister leave out the word *obey* from the vows. A short time later, she also asked people to call her Elizabeth Cady Stanton, not Mrs. Henry Stanton.

Elizabeth knew that by law she wasn't Henry's equal. But she would do everything she could to show her abilities and independence. Such ideas shocked Elizabeth's parents. No one in the Cady family attended the wedding, but after the ceremony Madge traveled with the couple to New York. Just eleven days after their marriage, Elizabeth and Henry sailed for London.

At the boardinghouse in London and at the convention, Elizabeth met all kinds of abolitionists. She met people who refused to buy anything produced by slave labor. She met people who favored sending black slaves to Africa. Still others, like her husband, called themselves "immediatists," because they wanted slaves to be freed immediately. But Elizabeth found it hard to put a label on one delegate.

At forty-six, Mrs. Lucretia Mott was a plain woman who wore the simple gray clothes that were favored by the Society of Friends, or Quakers. Elizabeth, at twenty-four, knew little of the world beyond school, balls, the Cady house in Johnstown, and her friends at Peterboro. But Lucretia was an experienced and mature woman. She was a minister in the Quaker church, one of the only churches that allowed women to serve. With her husband's support, Lucretia spoke out against slavery and other injustices. She had even dared to speak before mixed crowds of women and men outside her church.

Elizabeth admired Lucretia but worried about the impression she was making on her new friend. Lucretia rarely spoke, Elizabeth noticed, unless she had something important to say. Elizabeth herself sometimes found it impossible not to talk, whether she had anything to say or not.

But in spite of their differences, Lucretia and Elizabeth became friends. Writing in her diary one evening during the convention, Lucretia jotted, "Elizabeth Stanton growing daily in our affections."

Elizabeth and Lucretia soon discovered that they would have plenty of time to get to know each other better. The convention, it turned out, was not meant to be a gathering of *all* delegates from antislavery organizations, but only a gathering of *all male* delegates.

Even before the convention began, delegates were

arguing over whether to allow women to take part in the meetings and debates. Antislavery groups in Europe generally didn't allow women to belong. But some American groups welcomed women. These groups, along with all-female groups, had sent women to the convention.

When Lucretia Mott and the other women delegates arrived at the hall, they were hastily seated to the side, in a small, curtained-off area. Elizabeth sat next to Lucretia and listened to the male delegates make speeches for or against the women.

She was pleased when Henry defended the women and asked that they be seated with the men. But she had a hard time hiding her indignation when an English clergyman held up the Bible and declared that women were inferior to men. She'd heard such claims before, but she didn't expect to hear them at a convention about freedom and justice.

When another delegate rose from his seat, Elizabeth wanted to cheer. With a voice like thunder, he asked the clergyman to prove that the Bible said half the people of the world should be ruled by the other half. If such a thing could be proven, he argued, then they should gather all the Bibles in a pile and light a match to them. After all, hadn't they come to London to stop one half of the world from enslaving the other half?

Elizabeth couldn't understand how delegates could be in favor of freeing slaves while they were against letting women abolitionists work for the cause. And she wasn't alone. Each night at dinner, Elizabeth and the women delegates made sure the men heard their views. (One male delegate finally moved out of the boardinghouse where Elizabeth and Lucretia were staying. He wanted some peace.)

At the convention and on sightseeing trips around London, Elizabeth always managed to find a place next to Lucretia Mott. Lucretia was so far ahead of her time that she said out loud things Elizabeth had only dared think. According to Lucretia, a woman had just as great a right to hold an opinion as a man. And women had the right—and the duty—to act on their beliefs.

When Lucretia was asked to give a sermon on the slavery question at a church in London, Elizabeth went along. People squeezed into the pews. It was the first time Elizabeth and many of the others in the crowd had seen a woman speak in public.

Surely, Elizabeth thought, Lucretia was equal to or better than the male delegates. And surely, Lucretia Mott was not the only woman with something important to say. While the convention went on without Lucretia or any other woman, Elizabeth's anger grew.

She was even angrier about the way the women were being treated than she was about slavery. Growing up in the North, she had never experienced slavery directly, but she did know about unfairness toward women.

Elizabeth and Lucretia left the convention arm in arm at the end of a day of debates. Walking toward their boardinghouse, they decided to hold a convention of their own, as soon as possible. They would call for delegates to debate a question just as important as slavery—the question of equal rights for women.

④

Home and Beyond

Elizabeth kept in touch with Lucretia through letters and brief meetings after the World Anti-Slavery Convention. But the two women didn't organize a convention of their own. Lucretia was willing, but Elizabeth was busy with babies and moves.

When Elizabeth and Henry returned to the United States, they weren't sure at first where home would be. Henry didn't have a house of his own. And as Judge Cady and Edward Bayard had warned, Henry Stanton didn't earn enough money as a lecturer to support a family.

After much discussion, Elizabeth and Henry moved into the Cady home. Henry studied law under Judge Cady, but he didn't lose interest in abolition and other causes that the judge opposed. Throughout the 1840s,

Henry traveled often, working to elect abolitionists to the state legislature and the Congress.

When Henry traveled, Elizabeth was lonely, at first. In March 1842, the couple's first child, Daniel, was born. Daniel was named after Elizabeth's father, but the lively baby couldn't have been less like Judge Cady. Soon Daniel was shortened to Neil. Henry junior, nicknamed Kit, was born in the Cadys' house in Albany, where the Stantons lived for a short time. By the time Gat, or Gerrit Smith Stanton, was born in 1845, the family had moved to Boston.

To Elizabeth, being a mother was completely absorbing. She read everything she could find on raising children and then tried out theories of her own. Elizabeth felt so strongly about her theories that she often shared them with other parents, whether they were interested or not.

In Boston the Stantons rented a small house, their first as a couple. Some of the most famous abolitionists, preachers, and writers of the day came there for dinner. The poet Ralph Waldo Emerson was a frequent visitor and a close family friend. Frederick Douglass, a great African-American abolitionist, often shared the Stanton table. Elizabeth, who was used to the good cooks at the Cady home, knew the food was nothing special. But she and Henry both tried to make up for it with conversation. For his part, Henry was proud to have a wife who could talk intelligently on important topics.

Many of the Stantons' guests shared Elizabeth's interest in the rights of women. Paulina Davis, a wealthy widow from New York State, had tried to persuade the legislators in Albany to pass laws protecting the right of women to own property. Both Abby Kelly and Lydia Maria Child had sat with Elizabeth and Lucretia in the women's section at the World Anti-Slavery Convention, and they hadn't forgotten their indignation. Frederick Douglass was most interested in freeing his brothers and sisters in slavery, but he listened with interest and sympathy to Elizabeth's arguments on freeing women from the slavery of bad laws.

Elizabeth thought the dinnertime debates and discussions were better than food. But Henry wasn't so happy in Boston. He was trying to start a political career, and it was at a standstill. Lung problems, which he blamed on damp air from Boston Harbor, left him coughing and weak.

In 1847 Henry went to Seneca Falls, a small town at the head of Cayuga Lake in upstate New York. He was looking for a healthier place to live and new ground for both his law practice and political career.

Convinced that he had found both, he wrote to Elizabeth in June, summoning her and the boys to follow.

By the end of the month, Elizabeth was supervising the move into 32 Washington Street, Seneca Falls, New York. Judge Cady had given the house to Elizabeth on what was almost a dare. No one had lived in the big old place for five years. The roof sagged and mice played from the cellar to the attic. "You believe in woman's capacity to do and dare," the judge told his daughter, "now go ahead and put your place in order."

Putting this particular place in order was harder than Elizabeth had imagined. Since Henry traveled, he couldn't supervise the household or the repairs. Instead, Elizabeth took charge, sometimes with surprising results. Each time Henry returned to Seneca Falls, he scanned the house on Washington Street for changes. He liked to joke that his wife put in a new window whenever he was out of town, but he was pleased with her efforts.

Elizabeth felt she made a success of the repairs, but finding good servants was harder. Having grown up in a well-to-do family, Elizabeth counted on cooks and nursemaids to help with the housework. But in Seneca Falls, she had little or no help and three very hard-to-control boys.

The boys didn't mean to make trouble, but they did. There was the time Neil shot Gat in the eye with a homemade arrow. There was the time Neil shut his other brother in the smokehouse and "accidentally" locked the door. Then there was the day neighbors stopped by to let Elizabeth know that her youngest was crying. And no wonder, he had been left by his brothers—on the roof.

While battling her "young savages," Elizabeth also tried to keep the house clean and do the shopping, much of the cooking, all of the canning, and the weekly laundry. With no one to help her, keeping house and raising children weren't as fun as they had seemed back in Boston.

For the first time in her life, Elizabeth began to feel what ordinary women and mothers felt. Cooking, cleaning, and calling after the boys left her all tired out. Henry was away arguing cases or taking care of business for his clients for weeks out of each month. He wrote regularly, but letters were poor company for Elizabeth. Far from friends and family, she began to feel terribly alone.

The Stanton house was at the edge of Seneca Falls, where the streets turned into muddy ruts and sidewalks didn't exist. Elizabeth's closest neighbors were Irish immigrants who worked in the town's factories and mills. The women struggled with caring for their big families at home, while their husbands often drank their earnings away in the taverns. When the men came home drunk and angry, as they sometimes did, the children would run up Washington Street to Elizabeth for help.

As tired and frustrated as Elizabeth felt, she knew the neighbor women had an even harder time. At times their situations seemed hopeless. Elizabeth urged the men to take the temperance pledge and stop drinking. But she could do little for the women except to give them sympathy and advice.

About a year after the Stantons moved to Seneca Falls, Elizabeth's old friend Lucretia Mott arrived in nearby Waterloo, New York. Lucretia was there for a meeting of the Society of Friends. She was the guest of Jane and Richard Hunt, a Quaker couple. Jane Hunt invited Elizabeth to spend the afternoon visiting with Lucretia, along with Lucretia's sister Martha Coffin Wright and another Waterloo Quaker, Mary M'Clintock. Elizabeth hadn't realized how much she'd missed Lucretia until she sat down next to her and squeezed her hand.

Jane offered tea all around. At first the conversation was newsy and polite. But then Elizabeth began to speak. What she said surprised even herself.

Words poured out hot and quick. She was, Elizabeth told Lucretia and her friends, angry and upset about the way the women in her neighborhood were being treated. She was frustrated at not being able to do more to help. She was also tired of having nothing more interesting to do in her life than take the laundry out to dry while her husband traveled and took cases to court.

Women, Elizabeth argued, had the same right to a happy life as men, the same right to own property as men, the same right to a good education as men, the same right to be preachers and lawyers as men.

Lucretia and the others nodded. They thought Elizabeth quite brave to say such things. Mr. Hunt, who was listening from the next room, thought so too. Sticking his head in briefly, he agreed that women were often treated unfairly. But talking among themselves would change nothing. Why not do something about it?

Eight years had passed since Elizabeth had spoken with Lucretia about holding a convention for women. Elizabeth had been younger then, and more than a little in awe of Lucretia. Now, Elizabeth Cady Stanton was a grown woman of thirty-two. Looking at the eager faces around her, she knew the time was right. Before night fell, the women had written a notice to be placed in the next issue of the *Seneca County Courier:*

WOMAN'S RIGHTS CONVENTION.—A Convention to discuss the social, civil, and religious condition and rights of woman, will be held in the Wesleyan Chapel, at Seneca Falls, N.Y., on Wednesday and Thursday, the 19th and 20th of July, current; commencing at 10 o'clock A.M. During the first day the meeting will be exclusively for women, who are earnestly invited to attend. The public generally are invited to be present on the second day, when Lucretia Mott of Philadelphia, and other ladies and gentlemen, will address the convention.

(5)

Seneca Falls, 1848

A date, a time, a place, and a well-known speaker. Now all the women had to do was organize the convention. But what a task that would be! It was something none of them had ever done before. First they agreed to meet in a few days' time to put together a "Declaration of Sentiments," or an outline of all they believed.

This kind of declaration was common in those days. Temperance leagues, abolitionist groups, and reform clubs generally published a short declaration. When the women gathered again, this time around the parlor table at Mary M'Clintock's home, they faced a blank sheet of paper. Where would they begin?

It was common enough for women to be frustrated and unhappy with their lot—that was the reason for the convention, after all. But it was quite another thing to take their anger and sense of injustice and put it all into words for the world to see.

The women had almost given up when someone said, "We hold these truths to be self-evident, that all men *and women* are created equal. . . ." Of course! The Delaration of Independence would give them just the right framework. When the declaration was written in the 1770s, the founders of our country were declaring their independence from an English king who had treated them unfairly. All Elizabeth and her friends needed to do was to replace the old ruler's name, *King George,* with *all men.*

The authors of the Declaration of Independence had tacked on several resolutions, and Elizabeth was determined that the women would find an equal number of points to resolve. The day wore on as Elizabeth, Lucretia, Mary, Martha, and Jane searched their minds and the lawbooks for examples of injustice toward women.

Some were easy to come by. All of the women had been forced to live under laws they couldn't vote on or change. Some of them had seen divorce cases where the court gave the father custody of the children, whether he was a good father or a drunkard. And Elizabeth thought back to her father's office and the property laws that made women like Flora Campbell cry.

She remembered how left out she had felt when the boys from Johnstown Academy had gone off to college without her. Lucretia, who was a minister in her own church, knew that other churches were unfairly keeping women out of the ministry.

Both Elizabeth and Lucretia remembered being forced to sit on the sidelines during the World Anti-Slavery Convention. It was unfair, they resolved, for men to decide where women could sit and what they could do.

It was unfair, too, for women to be made so dependent. Since they had so few rights, women depended on men for almost everything. Elizabeth and the others at the M'Clintock house were lucky. They were married to men who supported them in all they wanted to do. But what about women who struggled to keep their families together when their husbands drank their wages? What about women like Flora Campbell who worked all their lives only to be treated like unwelcome guests in their own homes?

Once the ink had dried on the last word, the women sat back to relax and laugh. What had *they,* five respectable old married ladies, gotten themselves into? They would know for certain in a few days.

The mercury rose to ninety degrees on July 19, 1848. Around Seneca Falls, farmers were busy with an early harvest. Most people were busy with some kind of work by six o'clock that morning. But some, even those who had work to do, took a day off to go to the women's convention.

By nine-thirty a small crowd was milling about on Mynderse Street in front of the Wesleyan Chapel. Traveling in farm wagons, by carriage, on horseback, or on foot, they had come from as far as forty miles away. Some were Elizabeth's friends and neighbors from Seneca Falls. Most of the members of the Quaker church in Waterloo were there too. In the crowd were farm girls, young women who did sewing in their homes, mothers, and many children.

Elizabeth arrived just before ten, carrying a hefty volume or two of the laws of New York and the convention's declaration and resolutions. Henry Stanton was out of town, and Elizabeth wasn't saying if it was because of business or because he disapproved. (Family and friends hinted that Henry wasn't pleased with Elizabeth's newest interest. It was one thing for a wife to carry on smart dinner conversations; having a wife who spoke to crowds was something Henry wouldn't openly support.)

Still, some men had come to the convention. They

weren't invited until the second day, but Elizabeth and the others decided not to turn them away. They might be of some use.

Elizabeth's nephew proved useful almost right away. The person who was supposed to bring the key to the chapel never arrived. When the organizers despaired of ever getting in, the boy was boosted through a high, half-open window to unbolt the doors.

Inside, a film of dust from the unpaved street coated the windows and some of the wooden benches. Women, men, and children filed in, taking their seats on the main floor or in the gallery on three sides. Where the Wesleyan minister would normally preach there was a table, empty for the moment.

It was a matter of some embarrassment to Elizabeth, Lucretia, and the others, but none of them felt ready to lead the convention. They had never heard a woman call a convention to order, and they weren't sure that they could do it themselves. Spectators leaned forward to watch the knot of women in deep discussion by the table.

Finally, the women asked James Mott, Lucretia's husband, to lead the convention. Mary's daughter Mary Ann would be the secretary, and Elizabeth would be the first speaker. By eleven o'clock the world's first convention on women's rights had begun.

Speaking only barely loud enough to be heard, Elizabeth began, "We have met here today to discuss our rights and wrongs, civil and political. . . ." Lucretia followed with a speech on how women had been treated throughout history. She also read a funny story on women's rights that Martha had written but hadn't dared read aloud.

Not all of the organizers were brave enough to speak in public in front of a crowd of women and men. Those who did speak knew they would hear about it later from friends and neighbors. Not much had changed since Elizabeth's childhood. Most people still disapproved of women who spoke in public. It wasn't ladylike, people said. It might even be unnatural. Some of the women in the audience shifted uncomfortably in their seats as Lucretia and Elizabeth took turns speaking.

When Elizabeth again took the floor, her voice carried to the back benches. "The history of mankind is a history of repeated injuries and usurpations on the part of man toward woman," she read from the declaration. To prove the point, she read on about women who couldn't own property, about women who couldn't change laws because they couldn't vote, and about women who wanted to be doctors, lawyers, and ministers but never got the chance.

Elizabeth's words rose to the gallery when she continued through the resolutions, *"Resolved,* That woman is man's equal—was intended to be so by the Creator. . . . *Resolved,* That it is the duty of the women of this country to secure themselves their sacred right to the elective franchise. . . ."

When Elizabeth invited everyone to debate what she'd read, the part about elective franchise, or the right to vote, was pounced upon. Votes for women! Mrs. Stanton couldn't be serious, said people in the back pews. While the other resolutions were discussed and agreed upon, this one was debated into the second day, when men were encouraged to take part.

To some, asking for the vote was asking for too much too soon. But Elizabeth believed that if women were ever going to be considered as good as men, they needed to be able to vote on laws that affected them.

Speaking to the convention, she explained that women might feel differently if only good and sensible men could vote. "But to have drunkards, idiots, horseracing rum-selling rowdies, ignorant foreigners, and silly boys fully recognized, while we ourselves are thrust out from all the rights that belong to citizens, is too grossly insulting. . . ." Elizabeth had never spoken so strongly in her life: she apologized later in the day for her unladylike behavior.

Frederick Douglass, however, wasn't hearing any apologies for strong talk. He couldn't agree with Elizabeth more. Fairness and justice, he maintained, shouldn't depend on the color of your skin or whether you were born a man or a woman. Young children and adults leaned forward to hear Douglass speak.

Elizabeth was thrilled by his words. She wasn't surprised that a man who had once been a slave could understand the frustration of women. Both women and slaves were searching for freedom. When the final vote was taken, the declaration and resolutions passed with all present in favor.

It was late in the evening of the second day when the last speech ended. Nearly three hundred people had listened to eighteen hours of debate and discussion on women's rights and wrongs. Sixty-eight women and thirty-two men went one step further and signed their names to the declaration of sentiments.

Elizabeth Cady Stanton signed her name fourth, after Lucretia, Elizabeth's sister Harriet, and Margaret Prior of Seneca Falls. By signing her name, Elizabeth took her first step on a long road that would take her many miles from Seneca Falls. When the convention had ended, Elizabeth was tired but excited. She knew she had only begun to speak out on the rights and wrongs of women. Her journey had just begun.

Afterword

Elizabeth and the other signers of the declaration were laughed at from one end of the country to the other. Newspapers made fun of every aspect of the convention, from the resolutions to the organizers (who they said were five sour old maids). Judge Cady never quite forgave his daughter. He thought she'd made a fool of herself, and of him. Henry wasn't pleased, but he knew better than to try to stop Elizabeth.

He could slow her down, however. Both Henry Stanton and Judge Cady pressured Elizabeth to stop speaking in public. The wealthy Judge Cady let it be known that he was considering changing his will—and leaving Elizabeth out. Henry argued that Elizabeth couldn't be both a good mother and a good speech maker. By 1859 the couple had seven children. Henry told Elizabeth that the children needed their mother at home, not at women's rights conventions.

Despite these obstacles, Elizabeth Cady Stanton led the campaign for equal rights for women in the United States for more than fifty years. When she had first poured out her frustrations at Jane Hunt's house, Elizabeth was saying what many women felt. And when she had urged the women at the tea table to organize a convention, she was asking them to do something whose time had come.

Other conventions were held in cities and towns across the country. Elizabeth couldn't always go to the conventions, but she wrote letters to urge the women on. Through these letters, written by lamplight after her children were finally to bed, she became part of a world beyond Seneca Falls.

In 1852 Elizabeth met a schoolteacher named Susan B. Anthony. Susan was independent and unmarried and could travel when Elizabeth couldn't. Armed with Elizabeth's speeches, Susan became a powerful force for women's rights.

After her children were grown, Elizabeth spent about eight months out of every year crisscrossing the country as a lecturer. She wrote articles and books and directed a national women's group. And until her death in 1902, she took part in the many petition drives that helped pass laws to put women's wrongs to right.

Elizabeth Cady Stanton's signature is still there on the yellowed pages of petitions for women's property laws, for women's right to vote, and for fairer treatment of women in divorce cases. And her work can still be seen each time a woman votes, goes to college, argues a case in court, or treasures a favorite necklace or bracelet.

Bibliography

Banner, Lois W. *Elizabeth Cady Stanton: A Radical for Woman's Rights.* Boston: Little, Brown and Company, 1980.

Buhle, Mari Jo, and Paul Buhle, eds. *The Concise History of Woman Suffrage.* Urbana: University of Illinois Press, 1978.

Bull, Mary Bascomb. "Woman's Rights and Other 'Reforms' in Seneca Falls: A Contemporary View." Ed. Robert E. Riegel. *New York History* 46 (January 1965): 41–59.

Dorr, Rheta Louise Childe. *Susan B. Anthony: the Woman Who Changed the Mind of a Nation.* New York: Frederick A. Stokes Company, 1928.

Flexner, Eleanor. *Century of Struggle: the Woman's Rights Movement in the United States.* Cambridge: The Belknap Press, 1975.

Forster, Margaret. *Significant Sisters: The Grassroots of Active Feminism, 1839–1939.* New York: Knopf, 1985.

Griffith, Elisabeth. *In Her Own Right: The Life of Elizabeth Cady Stanton.* New York: Oxford University Press, 1984.

Gurko, Miriam. *The Ladies of Seneca Falls: The Birth of the Woman's Rights Movement.* New York: Schocken, 1976.

Lutz, Alma. *Created Equal: A Biography of Elizabeth Cady Stanton, 1815-1902.* New York: John Day, 1940.

Stanton, Elizabeth Cady. *Eighty Years & More (1815–1897): Reminiscences of Elizabeth Cady Stanton.* 1898. Reprint, New York: Schocken Books, 1971.

Stanton, Elizabeth Cady. "Reminiscences of Elizabeth Cady Stanton." Political Equality Club of Minneapolis, Minnesota Historical Society.

Stanton, Elizabeth Cady, Susan B. Anthony, and Matilda Joslyn Gage, eds. *The History of Woman Suffrage.* 6 vols. New York: Fowler & Wells, 1881–86. (Reprint available.)

Stanton, Theodore, and Harriot Stanton Blatch, eds. *Elizabeth Cady Stanton as Revealed in Her Letters, Diary, and Reminiscences.* 2 vols. New York: Harper & Brothers, 1922.

Weber, Sandra S. *Special History Study: Women's Rights National Historical Park, Seneca Falls, New York.* U.S. Department of the Interior/National Park Service, September 1985.

Index

engagement to Henry Stanton, 28, 30–31; friendship with Lucretia Mott, 32, 37, 43; as a mother, 37, 38, 40, 42, 57, 59; organizing Women's Rights Convention, 36, 45–46, 47–49; as a public speaker, 53–54, 57, 59; as a student, 11, 13–14, 16, 22–23, 24–25; on women's rights, 20, 33–34, 36, 39, 45–46, 47–51, 53–54, 59

Stanton, Gerrit Smith ("Gat") (son), 38, 42

Stanton, Henry Brewster (husband), 28, 30–31, 33, 37–40, 50, 57

Stanton, Henry Jr. ("Kit") (son), 38, 42

Troy Female Seminary, 24–25

Underground Railroad, 27
Union College, 11, 17, 22

Wesleyan Chapel, 46, 50, 51
Willard, Emma, 24–25
Women: attending college, 22–23, 24–25, 45, 49, 53; as delegates, 32–36; as housewives, 40, 42–43, 49; and marriage, 19, 20–21, 31; owning property, 18–22, 39, 45, 49, 53; speaking in public, 20, 32, 34, 46, 51, 53–54, 57, 59; as voters, 20, 48, 53, 54

Women's Rights Convention, 50–56, 59; organizing, 36, 37, 45–46, 47–49, 59. *See also* Declaration of Sentiments

World Anti-Slavery Convention, 30–34, 37, 39, 49

Wright, Martha Coffin, 43, 45, 47–49, 53

Yost, Maria, 11